JOURNEY
into the
Desert

John Brown

OXFORD
UNIVERSITY PRESS

For my family

OXFORD
UNIVERSITY PRESS

Oxford New York

Auckland Bangkok Buenos Aires Cape Town Chennai
Dar es Salaam Delhi Hong Kong Istanbul Karachi Kolkata
Kuala Lumpur Madrid Melbourne Mexico City Mumbai Nairobi
São Paulo Shanghai Singapore Taipei Tokyo Toronto

with an associated company in Berlin

Published by Oxford University Press, Inc.,
198 Madison Avenue, New York, NY 10016
www.oup.com

Hardback ISBN 0–19–515777–X

1 3 5 7 9 10 8 6 4 2

Printed in Hong Kong

Contents

Life on the
Edge

▶ In the Sonoran Desert lots of plants have found ways of living in harsh conditions.

Deserts are places of extremes. During the day the rocks can get hot enough to fry an egg on, and at night it can be freezing cold. For most of the year deserts are very dry, with little or no rain falling. In many deserts, all the rain that falls in a year wouldn't be enough to fill a teacup.

Deserts are found in many parts of the world. The biggest is the Sahara Desert in North Africa, which is as big as the whole of the United States. The driest is the South American Atacama Desert, where in some parts it hasn't rained for hundreds of years. When we think of a desert, we might imagine mile after mile of rolling sand dunes, but in fact there are many different kinds of desert. Some deserts are rocky and mountainous, while others are flat and featureless.

▶ Deserts are not always hot. Parts of the Antarctic are very dry and there is little life.

Deserts aren't really deserted at all. Many different kinds of plants and animals live in deserts, but sometimes you have to look very hard to find them. The animals and plants that do live there have to be able to cope with the harsh environment, and they have found lots of clever ways of surviving.

▲ The Empty Quarter in Oman: miles of rolling sand dunes are what most people imagine when they think of deserts.

Humans find it very difficult to live in deserts. If we can't find shade, the powerful sun will burn our skin. When it is hot, humans keep cool by sweating, which means that our bodies lose lots of water. Even sitting in the shade, we would need to drink two or three big glasses of water a day.

▲ The plants in the Atacama Desert survive by using water contained in sea mist.

The desert we are going to make a journey to is called the Sonoran Desert. This covers a large area in the Southwest United States and northern Mexico.

Tools for
Survival

The desert is a beautiful place, but it can also be very hostile. So we have to plan our trip carefully and make sure we bring the right equipment.

▲ We will do all our cooking on this little stove, the heart of our outdoor kitchen.

We have a little stove for cooking and some simple food like bread, dried fruit, rice, and pasta. We don't have anything that you would normally keep in your fridge at home because we have no way of keeping things cool out here.

Our First Aid kit includes things like tweezers for pulling out cactus spines and bandages in case we get blisters from walking. Each of us has a flashlight and spare batteries, and we have binoculars and a camera—you never know what you might see.

▲ This ingenious filter will allow us to "clean" any water we might come across to make it safe to drink.

The most important item to bring on a desert camping trip is lots of water. When you are a long way from help, you must have enough water to keep you alive if something goes wrong. We have four big containers in the truck. We also have a little filter pump, so if we ran out of water, we could use this to make any supply we find safe for drinking. If you look in shady places, you can sometimes find puddles left over from rains, but we would need the filter to clean the water.

▶ Which way home? By carefully using our compass we will be able to find our way back to the camp.

We have lightweight clothes and wide-brimmed hats to keep the sun off during the day, and lots of sunscreen. It can get cold at night, so we have down-filled sleeping bags and fleece jackets. It is important to wear good strong boots when you are walking around in the desert to prevent sharp cactus spines from sticking into your feet.

Camera: The desert is so beautiful that you might want to carry a camera with you. Early morning and late afternoon are the best times to take photos.

Backpack: Make sure your backpack fits you properly and is comfortable to wear. When you pack it, put the items you need most near the top so they are easy to get to. Here, our water bottle is attached to the outside so we can quickly grab a drink.

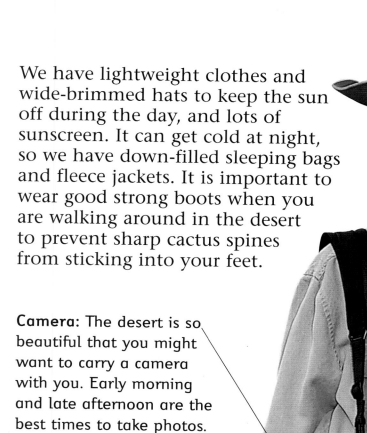

Hat: A wide-brimmed hat is essential for keeping the fierce sun off your head.

Binoculars: A good pair of binoculars is a must on an adventure like this. You never know what you might see in the desert.

Clothes: Dull colors are a good idea—they help you blend into the background and you might see wildlife before it sees you!

In the car there are two spare tires and a few other spares in case of a breakdown. We also have shovels to dig the car out just in case we get stuck in sand. We have left a note with friends giving details of where we are going and when we are planning to get back. So if we get into trouble, they will be able to organize a rescue.

Boots: You need tough boots to protect your feet against sharp rocks and those ever-present cactus spines.

Map of the
Journey

The Sonoran Desert covers an area of over 96,000 square miles. The character of the desert varies a lot. In some places the land is flat with just a few scrubby plants growing; in other places there are canyons with lush vegetation.

Large parts of the desert are very remote and not many people visit them. But in other places the desert is crisscrossed by busy roads and it feels like you are never far from a house or farm.

On our journey we want to experience the really wild desert, so we are going to have to drive a long way from town to find a campsite in the heart of the desert. We plan to camp for a few nights in one place and go on several small journeys on foot to explore the area. It is much more exciting to set out on foot: we are much more likely to see animals and really feel like we are experiencing the desert.

On the way home we'll make a detour to visit the Grand Canyon and see some American Indian ruins.

Grand Canyon

Volcano Crater

Box Canyon

Petroglyphs

Indian dwellings

City

Campsite

Night walk

From Skyscrapers to Saguaros

We fly into a big North American city, a mass of buildings sprawling for miles into the desert. We pick up our baggage and meet the friends who will be traveling with us. As we walk out though the doors of the airport into the sunshine, I'm hit by a wall of hot air. It's like walking into a big oven. I've never been anywhere this hot before.

▶ The desert comes right to the edge of the busy city. We quickly find the right road out of town and head off.

After loading all our equipment into the car, we head out of town to start our adventure. Soon we leave the busy city streets behind and find ourselves out in the desert. The road stretches ahead of us all the way to the horizon. At first the journey is easy, as the roads are smooth, but the further we drive from the city, the rougher the road becomes. Our car has a powerful engine and four-wheel drive, so we can cross sandy riverbeds and climb steep rocky paths. As the road gets bumpier, we have to drive more slowly and hold on tight. It's like being on a roller coaster ride.

Even the thick tires of our car can get torn up by the sharp rocks. And sure enough, a back tire gets punctured and we have to stop. It only takes a few minutes to change the wheel, but already we are dripping with sweat. I put a wrench down in the full blast of the sun. Big mistake! When I try to pick it up, it is too hot to touch, and I have to wrap my hand in a cloth to put the wrench back in the toolkit.

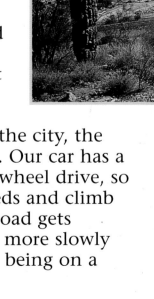

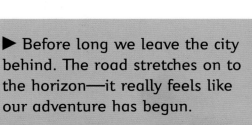
▶ Before long we leave the city behind. The road stretches on to the horizon—it really feels like our adventure has begun.

10

After driving for three hours, the city could be a million miles away. Not another human being in sight. Tired after the journey, we start searching for a campsite.

▶ The going is getting rough. Every now and again we stop to check that all our gear is safely secured in the back of the truck.

Home under the Stars

Choosing the right place for a campsite is always very important. We look for an area that is smooth and flat so it will be easy to set up our tents—but not a dry riverbed. That could be dangerous: if there is a heavy storm, water could come rushing down and wash us away.

We don't want to squash any small plants while we are walking around our camp and setting up our tents, so we look for an area that is just bare rock and sand. We must remember when choosing a campsite that when we leave to go home, there must be no trace that we were ever here. We will take home everything we brought with us and be careful not to disturb any of the plants or rocks around the camp. This helps to protect the desert and means that if someone else comes to camp here in the future, it will feel just as wild and new as it does to us now.

We find a good spot surrounded by saguaro cactuses and palo verde trees and park the truck in the shade. It's great to get out of the hot car and stretch our legs. It's amazing how quiet the desert is after the noise of the car—there is a gentle breeze and a few quiet bird calls in the distance. We unpack our equipment from the car and tie a piece of canvas between two trees to make a little shelter to store our gear under.

◀ It doesn't take long to put our tents up, and our home in the desert is ready.

We each choose a spot to put our tent up. It's always useful to have a tent when camping. Tents provide cool shade during the heat of the day and will keep us dry if there is a sudden summer storm. But one of the best things about camping in the desert is sleeping out under the stars. We unroll our sleeping mats on the bare ground outside our tents.

An inquisitive ground squirrel climbs to the top of a nearby cactus to watch us. I'm not quite sure if she likes her new neighbors—she gives an angry call and scampers off. We check carefully under nearby rocks for scorpions and snakes, and make sure we are not close to any ant nests. We don't want any uninvited guests in our camp!

◀ Meet the neighbors: this ground squirrel watches from a nearby cactus as we set up our camp.

▶ A long way from the busy city, this part of the desert probably hasn't changed for thousands of years. Here you can see the skeleton of a huge saguaro lying where it fell.

A Family in an Eggshell

O nce we have set up camp, we go for a quick walk to see what we can find. The desert we have come to is very special: while it gets very hot during the summer—up to 120 °F— it can be cold enough to snow in the winter. It is very strange to see cactuses with snow on them!

Some years it never rains, and the desert seems dead and baked by the sun. But if the rains are good, the desert can be transformed for a few weeks into a beautiful green paradise. We are visiting the desert at the start of the summer. There have been good rains in the winter. The plants are looking green, and in some places the desert floor is covered in wild flowers.

▲ After it has rained, even the most delicate plants can survive in the desert.

◀ This female Anna's hummingbird has just returned to the nest. Her chick is waiting to be fed a meal of tiny flies.

Suddenly a tiny bird shoots toward us like an arrow and hovers just inches away from us. Her wings are moving so fast that they are a blur. The hummingbird squeaks angrily at us before zooming off into the desert.

We walk slowly to the tree that she came from and search for what she was guarding. After looking carefully, we find a tiny little eggshell-shaped nest made from spider webs and animal hair. Hummingbirds use the sticky webs to glue the nest together, and they often add twigs and leaves to the outside to camouflage it.

Inside the nest there are two miniature, and rather strange-looking, baby birds. As we stand on our tiptoes to look in, they stick their heads out of the nest and cheep at us, maybe thinking that we are their mother coming back with food for them.

We take a few steps back and wait quietly. In a few minutes the mother returns with a beak full of tiny flies and feeds her chicks. She sticks her long, thin bill deep down their throats to give them food. Ouch!—it looks like it must hurt. But the chicks seem to enjoy it, and noisily demand more.

◀ There are lots of different plants in the Sonoran Desert, from tiny herbs to giant cactuses.

Plants that
Bite

Lots of the plants in the Sonoran Desert are cactuses. They have all found ways of living in this incredibly harsh environment. They can store lots of water in their bodies to survive droughts. Their tough skin is often pleated like a paper fan, which allows them to expand and fill with water when it rains. They are also covered in sharp spines to stop animals from eating them.

◄ Cholla cactuses are made up of sections that seem to jump out and bite you if you brush past them.

Cholla cactuses have the sharpest spines of all, with tiny little barbs on them so they stick in your skin. As I walk past a cholla, I accidentally brush the tips of the spines, and before I know it a segment of the cactus has come off and stuck to my arm. It is very painful, and I can't pull it off with my other hand or that will get stuck too. I get my penknife out of my pocket and gently pry it off. Yeow! No wonder it's called the jumping cholla cactus—it's as if it jumped out and bit me!

◄ Cholla cactuses can "travel" across the desert and colonize new areas by attaching themselves to passing animals—or feet!

▲ The pleats in the skin of the barrel cactus allow it to expand with water when it rains.

You might think that, if you ran out of water in the desert, you could cut into a cactus and drink the water it stores in its body. But with most cactuses you would get very sick if you did this. Only the barrel cactus contains water that humans can safely drink. Luckily barrel cactuses are common and easy to recognize. And if you do try to get a drink from one—watch its spines!

▶ The claret cup cactus has large flowers. These are visited by bees that feed on the nectar they hold.

The prickly pear has tiny little spines that grow around the base of its bigger spines. You can hardly see them, but if they get onto your skin, they can make you itch for days.

If you scratch into the surface of the hot desert ground, you'll almost certainly find a tangled network of cactus roots. The rains in the desert usually make only the top inch or two of soil damp, so cactuses don't have deep roots. Instead they spread their shallow roots over huge areas. The roots from a single cholla cactus, less than three feet tall, were found to cover an area nearly the size of a tennis court!

Glowing Scorpions and Rattling Snakes

Many animals that live in deserts only manage to survive by hiding during the intense heat of the day. As it becomes darker and cooler, the desert begins to wake up, and we begin to hear lots of mysterious rustling noises from the undergrowth around camp. We decide to go for a night walk to see what we can find.

Some scorpions that live in the desert glow brightly when you shine ultraviolet light on them. We have a special ultraviolet flashlight to search for them. When we turn it on, the scorpions look like little stars dotted over the desert floor. They are out hunting for small insects, which they catch with their big pincers and then sting with their tail.

We have to be very careful walking around at night. This is the time when rattlesnakes come out to hunt. They are very well camouflaged and their venom could kill you. Rattlesnakes eat small mice. They lie in ambush next to the little paths that the mice use, and when one comes along, the snake strikes, injecting powerful venom through hollow, needle-like teeth.

◄ Through the pits (hollows) on their nose, rattlesnakes are able to detect their prey's body heat.

◄ When there is a full moon, it lights up the whole desert. Sometimes the light is even strong enough to throw shadows.

▲ Throughout the night we can hear the fluttering wing beats of bats as they visit flowers and chase insects.

There are more different kinds of rattlesnake in the Sonoran Desert than in any other part of the world. The most common is the western diamondback rattlesnake, which can grow to over six feet long and can be almost as thick as your leg! During the cold winter months rattlesnakes hibernate in caves. You can find as many as 30 rattlesnakes sleeping in the same cave, which they sometimes share with desert tortoises and even pack rats.

The snake follows the scent trail left by the dying mouse and then gobbles it up headfirst. Snakes can't chew and have to swallow everything they eat in one piece. Sometimes they even unhinge their jaws in order to fit the mouse in. One mouse can feed a rattlesnake for up to three weeks. And if a rattlesnake has just eaten a mouse, you can sometimes see a mouse-shaped lump in its body!

► Some scorpions glow under ultraviolet light.

Visit to Another World

Next morning we wake up early. Before we put our shoes on, we check inside for scorpions—after last night we know there are lots around! After a quick breakfast, we get out our map of the area. We have decided to explore a nearby canyon today. The trip might take most of the day, so we take a packed lunch and are careful to carry plenty of water bottles in our backpacks.

◀ In some places the canyon is deep enough to bury six school buses stacked on top of one another.

It is very difficult to get down into the canyon because the walls are so steep. We walk along the edge until we find an ancient rock carving called a petroglyph, which was carved hundreds of years ago by an American Indian. It is a signpost, pointing the only safe way down into the canyon. Slowly and carefully we climb down.

Finally we reach the bottom. It is cool and shady down in the canyon, not like the hot desert above. There are still a few pools of water down here from the last time it rained. We come across the footprints of a coyote. Perhaps she came down into the canyon in search of water.

▼ Animals like this coyote sometimes come down into the canyons to look for water.

▲ This petroglyph was carved by an American Indian to act as a signpost, showing the safe way down into the canyon.

◀ These canyons go on for miles—it would be easy to get lost. We have to be careful to remember how to get out.

Sometimes the canyon is very narrow and we can touch both sides; sometimes it opens out and there are big trees growing in the shade. As we are walking along one of the narrow sections, we see a huge dead tree trunk, jammed across the canyon high above our heads. If it rains heavily, water can come rushing down these canyons like a tidal wave, rolling along huge rocks and tree trunks.

We look at each other and realize we shouldn't stay down here for long. It could be very dangerous if it floods. We quickly walk back to the place where we climbed down. By now the sky has filled with dark clouds—it looks like there may be a storm coming. It's time to get out of the canyon, fast!

Desert Fireworks

▶ We can see the rain off in the distance before it reaches us.

▼ During the summer months thunderstorms can build very quickly. When the sky starts to darken like this, it's time to look for shelter.

These summer storms in the desert are breathtaking. Towering thunderclouds build during the day, gathering energy from the hot air rising from the desert. Gradually they get darker and lower. For a few minutes the air becomes totally still, like the desert is holding its breath. Then suddenly the wind comes, quickly followed by torrents of rain. It feels like the end of the world. Huge saguaro cactuses sway like they are made of rubber, while dust and leaves are caught up and blown into the air.

Lightning strikes all around us, lighting up the sky. The crash of thunder is terrifying, and we lie huddled inside our tents. It's good to be out of the rain. We quickly change into dry clothes and slowly start to warm up. Every time there is a lightning strike, we jump and silently count the seconds before the thunder, so we can tell how close the lightning strikes are.

▼ It is hard to believe in a desert, but winter storms can leave cactuses dusted in snow for a few hours before it melts.

▲ The Sonoran Desert is one of the best places on Earth to see lightning: the desert air is so hot and the clouds so high that the lightning has a long way to travel to reach the ground.

We climb back out of the canyon into the desert. There are threatening clouds gathering. This could be a big storm—we got out of the canyon just in time. Now it's a headlong rush back to camp to get our sleeping bags and equipment inside the tents. As we hurry back, the wind starts to rise and the first fat raindrops begin to fall onto the dry desert soil.

A Carpet of
Color

The next morning we are woken up before dawn by the eerie howling of coyotes. There is hardly a sign of last night's storm. The desert ground is so thirsty for water that it quickly soaks up the rain, and the air feels so fresh, as if the rain had washed it clean.

▶ The Mexican golden poppy grows, flowers and dies in a few short weeks after rain, but its seeds can survive in the soil for years.

The desert always looks special after rain, the plants respond so quickly. It has been a good rainy season this year, and in some places there are carpets of wild flowers. Thousands of beautiful and delicate plants are bursting forth from earth that is usually bare and too hot to touch.

Insects are buzzing everywhere. They are flitting about busily, gathering up pollen and nectar as quickly as they can. In a few weeks the desert will become parched and lifeless again, and it might not rain again for many years. The seeds these plants produce are like little time capsules, surviving for many years in the painfully hot desert earth, just waiting to spring into life next time it rains. It may be a long wait, as really good rains only occur about every ten years in the Sonoran Desert.

▲ For a few short weeks after rain, it is difficult to believe that this is a desert.

There are flowers of many different sizes, shapes, and colors. Some are shaped like dishes, making it easy for bees and other insects to land on them. Others are trumpet-shaped and are designed so that only the long tongues of hummingbirds can feed on the nectar they hold deep inside.

The desert is such a difficult place for plants to live that many cram the whole cycle of their lives into a few short weeks after it has rained. Plants like cactuses do the opposite, growing slowly over many years, but they are tough enough to survive those times when there is no rain.

Many desert plants that look dead during the heat of summer are actually still alive. When conditions are tough for these plants, they drop their leaves and go into a dormant (resting) state, waiting to burst into life next time it rains.

▶ Believe it or not, the buds of these pink flowers taste delicious when roasted!

Spineless
Wonders

The desert may appear to be devoid of animal life. But look closely amongst the plant stems and rocks and you will begin to find the world of arthropods—strange-looking creatures living even stranger lives.

▶ This giant desert centipede can grow to eight inches long. It is a ferocious predator and has been known to kill animals as big as mice.

Insects, spiders, scorpions, and centipedes —in fact, most of the animals we think of as "creepy-crawlies"—are arthropods. They have a tough outer covering to their bodies, like a little suit of armour, called an exoskeleton. Bees and many other types of insect can fly, while arthropods such as spiders and scorpions jump or walk. All adult insects have six legs, while millipedes can have over a hundred. Many arthropods eat plants, and some even eat other arthropods!

▲ Whip scorpions usually live in abandoned rodent burrows. They eat other arthropods, which they impale and crush with their powerful spiny forelimbs.

◀ This sun spider has caught a grasshopper. In relation to its body size, the jaws of the sun spider are among the largest and most powerful of any animal.

Arthropods are superbly adapted to live in deserts. Many can survive for months with very little food and virtually no water. Because arthropods are small, they can find lots of little cracks in rocks and tunnels to hide in during the heat of the day. Their exoskeleton is waterproof, so they don't lose precious moisture through their skin like mammals do.

Sun spiders are some of the most fearsome-looking arthropods you might meet in the Sonoran Desert. These creatures aren't true spiders but they look like them, and a big one would cover the palm of your hand…if you could ever summon up the courage to pick one up! They are predators: like miniature cheetahs, they run at high speed to catch their prey. They like to eat insects, spiders, and even lizards, which they kill with their powerful jaws.

On summer nights you might find another of the desert's hairy, eight-legged inhabitants out on the prowl. The male tarantula spends the first ten to twelve years of his life living in his silk-lined burrow, pouncing out now and again to catch unsuspecting prey that wanders past. Then, when he is old enough, he climbs out of his burrow and walks the desert, looking for a female to mate with.

You might think that an animal as formidable as a tarantula would have no arthropod enemies in the desert. But there is a kind of wasp, called a tarantula hawk, which is an expert at hunting tarantulas. These huge wasps sound like pocket-sized helicopters as they fly over the desert looking for tarantula holes. Once they have found a hole, they try to tempt the spider out so they can stun it with their sting. Then—like a scene from a horror film—they carry the paralyzed spider off to a burrow and lay an egg on its body. And when the wasp larva hatches, it has a live, eight-legged meal to feast on!

◀ This huge wasp could mean big trouble for an unwary tarantula.

Sentinels of the Desert

The most distinctive plant in the Sonoran Desert is the saguaro cactus. These incredible plants play a vital role in the life of the desert. Saguaros are among the giants of the plant world. They can grow as tall as a three-story house, weigh as much as two big cars and live to be over 200 years old.

◄ The saguaro cactus starts off life as a tiny seed, not much bigger than this full stop. Over hundreds of years it can grow as tall as a three-story house.

Saguaros can be very common in the Sonoran Desert, and in some places it can look like there are forests of these massive cactuses. There are not many trees that are able to survive in the harsh desert environment, so many birds build their nests in saguaros to keep their eggs away from the hot ground and safe from predators.

◄ Lots of animals love the sticky red fruit the saguaro produces in the summer. These two male longhorn beetles are not just feeding on the fruit, they are also waiting for a female to mate with. This kind of beetle uses saguaro fruit as a meeting place to mate!

In spring the tips of the arms of the saguaro cactus become covered in huge white and yellow flowers. Bats, birds, and a whole host of insects come to feed on the sweet nectar contained in the flowers. This is exactly what the saguaro wants: as these animals reach deep inside the flower to find the nectar, they brush past the male parts of the flower, which are laden with yellow pollen.

This pollen rubs off onto the animals, who then carry it off with them to fertilize the next flower they visit. When saguaros are flowering, you can sometimes see birds flying from one cactus to another looking like they had stuck their heads in yellow paint, there is so much pollen on them.

In the middle of summer, when the temperature soars and it seems like there is no food around, the saguaro cactus keeps the desert alive. It is at this time that it produces its fruit. Where once there were flowers on the tips of the cactus arms, now there are big, red, delicious fruits. All the animals of the desert from bats to beetles love this fruit. We find some on a low arm: it tastes a bit like strawberry jam, and it makes our tongues turn red!

▼ In spring these big white flowers grow on the tips of the saguaro's arms. You can see the yellow pollen inside the flower.

▶ This elf owl has made a nest inside a hole that a Gila woodpecker has hammered into the trunk of a giant saguaro.

Horned Lizards
and Harvesting Ants

As we are having breakfast, we notice that last night's storm has knocked some of the fruit off the top of a nearby saguaro. This windfall has been discovered by a colony of harvester ants, who are busy pulling the seeds out of the sticky fruit and carrying them back to their hole. They are working very hard to get all the seeds inside their nest before it gets too hot for them to stay out in the sun.

▲ This harvester ant is wrestling to pull a saguaro seed out from the fruit. Imagine trying to pull a football out of a giant-sized sticky gumdrop—with your teeth!

I notice something out of the corner of my eye. It looked like a rock moved! We take a closer look and realize that it isn't a rock but a horned lizard. An amazing little lizard, it is so well camouflaged that you can hardly see it against the pebbles and sand. Up close it looks like a miniature dinosaur.

These lizards have an amazing trick up their sleeve. Coyotes love to eat lizards, and if a coyote manages to see though a horned lizard's camouflage, the lizard is in big trouble. But if the coyote tries to bite the horned lizard, it squirts blood from its eyes into the coyote's mouth. The lizard's blood must taste disgusting to the coyote, which usually runs off in shock, giving the resourceful little lizard a chance to escape.

We watch the horned lizard having its ant breakfast as we finish ours.

◄ A few clouds remain after last night's storm; the morning air feels cool and clean.

▲ In slow motion we can see the horned lizard squirt blood from its eye.

Some kinds of horned lizard eat almost nothing but ants, which they gobble up with their sticky tongue. They dart around, and with each quick flick of their tongue another ant disappears. The ants try to fight back, but their strong jaws make no impression on this armored ant-eating machine. We look around and find the lizard's little black droppings. They crumble as you pick them up—they are made of nothing but the digested remains of dead ants!

► Resembling a miniature dinosaur, the horned lizard feasts on the ants. Look carefully and you can see an ant valiantly trying to fight back!

Roadrunners and Sky Wolves

When we think of birds in the desert, there is one character that springs to mind: the high-speed roadrunner, whose 'meep meep' call always means trouble for Wyle E. Coyote. You might be lucky enough to see a roadrunner darting around on the ground in search of food. These speedy birds don't often fly, but they can run at around 15 miles an hour—faster than most humans. They eat almost anything they can catch—small birds, mice, lizards, even snakes. Roadrunners have special black skin, which absorbs heat well. On cold mornings they lie in the sun, fluff their feathers up, and sunbathe to warm up before going hunting.

▲ This roadrunner has used speedy footwork to catch a lizard to eat.

Some other birds we often link with deserts are vultures. In western films we see them circling overhead, waiting for an unfortunate explorer to run out of water. Vultures might not feed on many explorers these days, but they still spend much of their day soaring above the desert in search of carrion—dead animals. They rely on their sharp eyes and keen sense of smell to find food. Not very appetizing to us, perhaps, but vultures play an important role in the desert by cleaning up the bodies of dead animals. Vultures don't have feathers on their heads like most birds. Instead there is just bare, wrinkled skin. Feathers would get horribly messy when the vulture sticks its head inside a dead animal to feed.

◀ Sharp eyes, keen smell, and a powerful beak help make the turkey vulture an excellent scavenger.

As we are driving along, we see several large birds perched on a saguaro. They must be Harris's hawks. These beautiful birds are predators, but unlike most predatory birds, they hunt in packs—like wolves of the air. Families of Harris's hawks work together to scare rabbits and other prey out into the open, where they can catch them more easily using their clever teamwork.

► This family of Harris's hawks has made its nest in a saguaro cactus.

▼ Harris's hawks use teamwork to catch their prey.

Meeting a
Monster

The plan for today is to walk to a volcano crater. It's a long walk, so we pack some lunch and lots of water. We set off early, and the air is still cool as we stroll across the desert. We have only been walking for a few minutes when we hear a noise.

Up ahead, a bird is flapping around the base of a cactus and squawking. As we approach, we can see there is a creature in the bird's nest. It is one of the world's most mysterious lizards, which scientists know very little about—the Gila monster.

This one is a big adult, and it has nearly finished making breakfast out of the bird's eggs. We sneak up close to the Gila monster to get a good look. It doesn't seem bothered by us, but we have to be careful not to get too close—this lizard could be dangerous. It is one of only two venomous lizards in the world, and its bite is incredibly painful.

◀ This Gila monster is feeding on birds' eggs, one of its favorite foods.

◀ This crater is over a mile across. There must have been a huge explosion when the volcano erupted.

▼ Mountain lions live in the more rugged areas of the Sonoran Desert. They are very shy and difficult to see.

We leave the monster and continue to climb up the volcano. We finally reach the top and look down. The crater is enormous. Millions of years ago molten rock rising from deep inside the Earth came into contact with wet rocks near the surface. The steam that formed caused an explosion like a giant bubble bursting, showering the surrounding desert with red-hot cinders.

In the cool of the evening we walk slowly back towards camp, enjoying the incredible scenery. Something catches our attention on a distant rocky cliff. Frozen to the spot, we hold our breath. There is a mountain lion walking slowly along a ridge. She hasn't seen us, but before we can reach for our binoculars, she is gone, bounding out of sight to begin her night's hunt for deer or bighorn sheep.

35

It doesn't seem like we've been asleep long when we are woken by a strange noise coming from somewhere out in the desert. It sounds like the racket from a hundred arcade games. Pulling on our clothes and grabbing our flashlights, we rush out to see what is going on. As we walk across the moonlit desert, the noise gets louder and louder. What can it be?

We come across a muddy puddle left over from last night's rain, and it is absolutely seething with hundreds of little toads. It seems like the ground around our feet is alive: more and more toads burst out from the soft, wet earth at the edge of the puddle and jump into the water to join the others.

◀ A forest of saguaros is silhouetted in front of the setting Sun. Only now does the desert start to cool down.

▼ You might only see a spadefoot toad on a few special nights of the year.

Toad Love and Shooting Stars

We get back to camp as it gets dark. It's been a great day, and we are excited, hungry, and tired. After cooking a big meal, we climb into our sleeping bags and quickly fall asleep.

These are spadefoot toads. They have been waiting, maybe for years, for a night like this—hiding underground, away from the dry heat of the desert, and hoping for the rains to come. As they come burrowing out of the soil, it is easy to see why they are called spadefoot toads: on their back feet there are hard pads, which they use like shovels to push through the desert earth.

Tonight the males are searching for females to mate with. The females will lay their strings of eggs in the puddle, and by morning all will have burrowed back underground again, leaving thousands of eggs behind them. The toads hope that their eggs will have enough time to hatch and develop into baby toads before the hot sun dries up their puddle.

The frantic activity continues for a long time, but finally things begin to calm down. Eventually, one by one, the toads, like miniature bulldozers, dig themselves back into the desert earth.

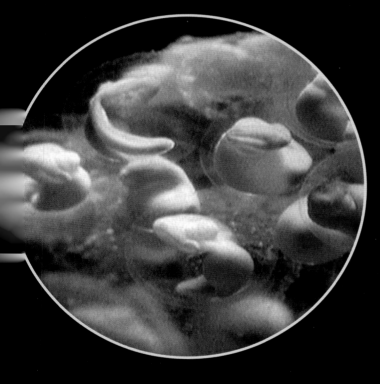

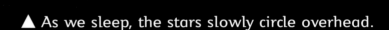
▲ As we sleep, the stars slowly circle overhead.

◄ The spadefoot toad eggs rush to develop: they can change from egg to baby toad in just two weeks!

Now we are really tired. We return to camp and get back into our sleeping bags. I lie on my back and look up at the sky, thinking of all the incredible things I have seen during these few days in the desert. I can see so many stars, scattered across the sky like a frozen firework. Just as I am dozing off, a shooting star whizzes across the sky. I make a wish to come back to the desert again soon.

➤ Summer storms trigger spadefoot toads to breed. Some individuals emerge, breed and then eat enough in one night to allow them to hide underground until the following year!

The Grand Canyon

Sadly it's time to leave the desert and head for home. We pack up our equipment, carefully checking that our campsite is the same as it was when we arrived. We have one last treat in store—a visit to the Grand Canyon.

▶ Vultures soar in the hot-air currents that well up from the bottom of the canyon.

This is one of the most famous and spectacular places on Earth. Over the past six million years the Colorado River has cut through layer after layer of rock to create a canyon that is over 300 miles long, over a mile deep in places, and as much as 10 miles wide. It would take you about three weeks to raft the canyon's whole length.

◀ The Colorado River slowly winds along the bottom of the Grand Canyon.

▼ Bighorn sheep graze on the plants growing on the steep slopes of the canyon.

We arrive at the canyon edge and rush out of the car to have a look. It's amazing! At the bottom of the canyon we can just see the glint of water, showing where the river flows. Huge cliffs of colored rock drop away from under us. It looks like some mighty giant has taken a slice through a huge layer cake.

Through my binoculars I can just see the tiny specks of people walking down a steep path that leads to the bottom of the canyon. The Grand Canyon is so deep and wide that it takes walkers three days to cross from one side to the other.

On the other side of the canyon we can just make out some bighorn sheep. These nimble-toed animals can run around on nearly vertical rock faces. They feel safe in the canyon because predators like mountain lions find it hard to catch them on the steep, treacherous slopes.

It is getting dark, and reluctantly we return to the car to go home.

◀ If you look carefully in the picture, you can just see where the river runs along the bottom of the canyon.

People of the
Desert

During our journey into the desert we have seen some wonderful plants and animals that have adapted to survive in this harsh environment. We can just imagine how difficult it would be for humans to live here. But people have managed to survive in the desert for thousands of years, expertly making use of the resources they found.

People first arrived here at least 12,000 years ago, when they would have shared their world with mammoths, saber-toothed cats, and giant sloths. At that time the weather was cooler and more rain would have fallen. Slowly the climate became hotter and drier, and many kinds of animal died out, but humans remained.

◄ Thousands of years ago we shared this wild desert landscape with mammoths, giant sloths, and saber-toothed cats.

◄ These beautiful cliff dwellings suggest that Native American cultures were well organized for life in the desert.

► "Newspaper Rock" is covered in hundreds of little pictures like this hunting scene. We are not sure what many of the symbols mean.

Today we can still find evidence of these Native American cultures in the desert. In some places there are whole cities built into the cliffs. It is thought that these cities were occupied for about 1,000 years, but then—suddenly and mysteriously— the people vanished. Perhaps there was a drought that killed all their crops and the people were forced to move on.

Farming was an important part of Native American life. Farmers developed ingenious ways of diverting river and rainwater into their fields to irrigate their crops. In some places you can still see the channels they constructed snaking for miles across the desert floor.

▼ Reconstruction of a hunting party from the past: American Indians would have worn clothes similar to these, which are made of animal skins and lightweight cloth.

In a shady canyon there is a place called Newspaper Rock, a slab of sandstone that is covered in Native American art. If you look closely, you can see pictures that show people hunting deer and sheep with bows and arrows. Native Americans were very skillful hunters, who crafted arrow tips and spearheads out of stone. You still might find one of these beautifully made and amazingly sharp spearheads on the desert floor.

Deserts under Threat

Deserts are very fragile webs of life: the existence of these ecosystems depends on a delicate balance between all the different plant and animal species that live there. Unfortunately, in some parts of the desert that balance has been upset by one species: humans. People are attracted to live in the Sonoran Desert by the promise of sunshine and beautiful scenery, but this means that the population of many desert cities is growing alarmingly.

▼ Bit by bit the desert is sold off for housing development, but what value can we attach to such a special place, and is it really ours to sell?

LOT FOR SALE
624-4732
$ 35,000 CASH

▲ Modern technology allows us to pump water from deep within the Earth up to the hot desert surface. But is this the right thing to do?

A hundred years ago the lack of water limited the number of people who could survive in the desert. But now we pump water from deep within the Earth or pipe it in from rivers hundreds of miles away. With this new supply of water, hundreds of miles of untouched desert have already been plowed for farming crops that would normally shrivel and die under the hot desert sun. In some areas, the demand for water has meant that the supplies of groundwater have already been used up. And it might be hundreds of years before they recover, if they ever do.

All the people who move to the desert need somewhere to live. Now miles of new houses stretch out over land that, only a few years ago, was beautiful desert. What has happened to the mountain lions and hummingbirds that once lived there?

▶ This saguaro stands as a lonely reminder of the beautiful desert that has been cleared to build these houses.

We have to ask ourselves what is more important. Should we be able to live in air-conditioned houses and have swimming pools in the desert—or should the animals and plants that lived here for thousands of years before people arrived be able to continue living in the desert, hopefully for thousands of years to come?

We were very careful to leave our little campsite in the desert exactly as we found it. We must also remember, as a society, to treat the whole desert in the same way. We do not own the desert, but it is entirely our responsibility to protect it for future generations.

► Which is more valuable: the wild desert or the sterile golf course that has replaced it?

Saving the *Deserts*

The Sonoran Desert faces many threats: its groundwater being used up to water crops and golf courses..., the growth of cities steadily eating into the wild areas where animals live..., the list goes on. So why do we need to protect wild places like the Sonoran Desert?

As our world gets busier and our cities get bigger, wild, untamed areas become increasingly valuable to us as human beings. It is an uplifting experience to visit places where there isn't any noise from cars or litter on the ground. And even if you can't visit these wild areas very often, it is comforting just to know that they are there.

◄ Shy and beautiful, mountain lions need large areas of unspoilt desert through which to roam, and we need mountain lions to remind us of the beauty of wild places.

▲ Could these flowers hold secrets that might cure diseases? Unless we protect the desert, we may never know.

Native Americans are very skilled at using the plants that grow in the desert as medicines. If we protect the desert and learn more about the plants that live there, there is a good chance that we will be able to find cures for some of our diseases. But if we destroy the last habitat of a rare plant to make way for more houses, then whatever secrets a plant may hold will be lost forever.

We are still learning about the animals and plants of the desert. We now know that in some places even the ground we walk on is alive. There is a thin crust of bacteria and algae, which stabilizes the surface of the desert so plants can grow. This crust is a vital piece of the desert ecosystem. It can take a hundred years to grow, but it can be destroyed with one footstep. The more we learn about each piece of an ecosystem, from tiny bacteria to the powerful mountain lion, the better we will be able to protect them.

The creation of parks means that, in many areas of the Sonoran Desert, no more roads or houses can be built, while still allowing people to go hiking and camping like we have just done. And laws now protect many of the desert creatures that are especially at risk.

We need to be sensitive to the environment and plan carefully for the future. If we do so, the animals and plants we have seen during our journey into the desert will still be living their remarkable lives for many, many years to come.

▲ Signposts warn hikers to keep to the path. In some places even the ground we walk on is alive.

▼ He was here first! We can live side by side with creatures like this, but we should always remember that this desert is his only home, and we must treat it with care.

Glossary

aestivation The way some animals spend the hottest and driest period of the year in a resting state. For example, spadefoot toads aestivate to avoid drying out.

amphibians A group of animals (vertebrates) that includes frogs, toads, and newts. They have moist skin, and most species need water in which to lay their soft eggs.

arachnids A large group of arthropods including scorpions and spiders. Their body is divided into two sections, with four pairs of legs attached to the front section.

arthropods A huge group of invertebrate animals that includes insects and arachnids. Arthropods' bodies are split into segments and covered in a tough exoskeleton.

Atacama Desert A desert in northern Chile, considered to be the driest place on Earth.

barrel cactus A short, squat cactus that looks like a barrel and has a pleated skin. Some types of barrel cactus contain water that is safe to drink, but you have to be very skillful to be able to extract the water.

cactuses A group of succulent plants adapted to live in arid (dry) regions. They are usually covered in spines and often have brightly colored flowers at certain times of year.

camouflage The way that some animals and plants have evolved (developed) to look like their surroundings in order to disguise themselves.

canyon A steep-sided river valley formed when a river erodes down through the rock. You could jump across some narrow canyons; others, such as the Grand Canyon, can be over 9 miles wide.

carnivore An animal or plant that feeds on animal material.

cholla cactus A type of cactus that grows in segments, new segments being added to the ends of its branches each rainy season. With some chollas, the segments are easily detached and, if they fall on the right soil, grow into a new plant.

conservation The way we try to manage the natural resources and maintain the correct balance of all the elements in an ecosystem, especially one that is under threat.

desert A place where there is very little water available, plants are usually widely separated, and animals develop clever strategies to survive the arid (dry) conditions.

dormancy (1) A stage in an animal or plant's life, such as hibernation or aestivation, when its life processes (metabolism) slow down. **(2)** The period during which certain healthy seeds will not germinate (send forth shoots) even if they are watered. This prevents all the seeds of a plant germinating at the same time, just in case there is a drought that might kill all the plants at once.

drought A long period without rain; moisture in the soil is reduced so much that plants suffer from lack of water.

ecosystem A community of animals and plants living together in a habitat and interacting as one unit.

erosion The processes that wear away the surface of the Earth. Wind, frost, and water can all cause erosion.

evolution The way that plants and animals slowly accumulate changes over generations under the influence of their environment. In the desert animals and plants have evolved to be able to cope with lack of rain.

exoskeleton The tough outer covering that arthropods have. The exoskeleton is shed at certain times to allow the animal to grow.

fruit The tissues that a plant forms around its seeds. Often the fruit is fleshy and delicious, so animals will eat the fruit and disperse the seeds.

groundwater The stores of water that have soaked through the soil and lie in the bedrock.

habitat The area occupied by a plant or animal.

herbivore An animal that feeds on plant material.

hibernation Spending the winter in a resting state. In the desert many reptiles avoid the coldest period of the winter by hibernating underground.

insects A huge and extremely varied group of arthropods. Adults usually have three sections to the body: head, thorax and abdomen, with 3 pairs of legs attached to the thorax. Many insects also have wings. So far over 1 million different kinds of insect have been discovered and named.

invertebrates Animals that do not have a backbone. Over 97 percent of all animal species, including arthropods, worms, and slugs, are invertebrates.

mammals A group of vertebrates, including humans and many large animals. Mammals produce milk to feed their young and are usually covered in hair. Sometimes called "warm-blooded," mammals can generate their own body heat and can cool themselves by sweating and panting.

Native Americans Descendants of the first people to arrive in North America from Asia at least 12,000 years ago. Also called American Indians. Many different groups of Native Americans live in North and South America.

Navajo An American Indian tribe that lives in some areas of the Sonoran Desert.

nectar A sugary liquid produced by some plants to tempt pollinators, such as humming-birds and butterflies, to visit their flowers.

nocturnal Active at night. Many desert animals are nocturnal to avoid the heat of the day.

petroglyphs Pictures carved into rock, usually by ancient peoples. Some seem to tell stories; others appear to act as "signposts." The meaning of many remains a mystery.

photosynthesis The chemical process that allows plants to make food from sunlight, water, and carbon dioxide. Oxygen is produced during this process and released into the air.

pollen Tiny grains produced by the male parts of flowers, which need to be transferred to the female parts of the flower to fertilize the eggs.

predator An animal that kills other animals for food.

prickly pear A kind of cactus made up of flat segments. The red fruit of many species is very tasty and can be eaten raw or made into juice and jam.

reptiles A group of vertebrates with scaly skins, including snakes, lizards, and dinosaurs. Unlike mammals, reptiles do not generate their own body heat. They bask in the sun to warm up and have to retreat into the shade when it gets too hot. Most reptiles lay eggs.

roots The part of a plant that is used to anchor the plant and absorb water and nutrients from the soil. In deserts rainwater doesn't penetrate deep into the soil, so most desert plants have their roots in the top 3 feet of soil.

saguaro cactus A characteristic plant of the Sonoran Desert, a huge, column-like cactus that can live for over 200 years.

Sahara Desert A vast desert in north Africa; the biggest desert in the world, covering 8 percent of the world's land area.

scavenger An animal that feeds on dead animal or plant material, rather than killing for food itself. Vultures are scavengers.

scorpions A group of arthropods. They usually live on the ground and are active at night, feeding on other arthropods. They have two pincers for catching and holding prey and a stinger at the end of their tail.

Sonoran Desert The desert our journey takes place in; an exceptionally rich and diverse desert in southwestern USA and northern Mexico.

succulent A type of plant, including cactuses, with special fleshy tissue designed to hold and conserve water.

ultraviolet light A color of light that humans can just barely see. Some animals, like bees, can see ultraviolet light clearly, and some flowers have special ultraviolet-colored lines on them to attract bees.

venom Chemicals produced by some animals that can be harmful to other animals, used to kill or subdue prey or to defend against attack.

vertebrates Animals that have a skull and a backbone. The group includes fish, birds, mammals, amphibians, and reptiles.

volcano A place where the molten core of the Earth has burst through to the Earth's surface sometimes violently, leaving a crater and covering the landscape with lava and cinders.

Index

Acknowledgments

Key: t – top, tl – top left, tr – top right, c – center, cl – center left, cr – center right, b – bottom, bl – bottom left, br – bottom right.

All photographs by John Brown, except the following, which are produced by kind permission of Oxford Scientific Films:

B. Bennett, p 32 bl; C. Brett, p 40 tr; J. Brown, pp 20 tr, 21 tr, 37 tr; Dr J. A. L. Cooke, pp 27, 32 t, 37 br; M. Cordano, pp 42 bl, 43 tr; D. J. Cox, pp 33 b, 44 bl; E. R. Degginger, pp 10–11; D. M. Dennis, cover tr, p 26 b; W. Faidley, p 23 t; M. Fogden, p 26 t; M. Hamblin, p 21 bl; M. Jones, p 38 t; Z. Leszczynski, p 16 b; A. Lister, p 4 b; J. MacDonald, p 19 tr; O. Newman, p 29 cr; J. Robinson, p 39 br; N. Rosing, cover c, p 35 br; R. Toms, p 42 tr.

John Brown would like to thank the following for modeling: Luke Godfrey, p 7; Bill, Joaquim, Lee and Rose, p 41. He would also like to thank Sean Morris, who read and checked the text.

Artwork on pp 8–9 by Sarah Young.